BISHOP JOSEPH STRICKLAND

Connecting the Church with the Wider World through Service

Robert A. Evans

1

Copyright

CONTENTS

PRESENTATION

In the core of the Ward of Tyler, Texas, a cleric arises as a convincing figure spanning the hallowed and mainstream — a shepherd profoundly dedicated to interfacing the Congregation with the more extensive world through the groundbreaking force of administration. This book dives into the life, authority, and significant effect of Cleric Joseph E. Strickland, a man whose excursion rises above the walls of conventional ministerial limits, contacting the more extensive local area with empathy, conviction, and an undaunted obligation to support.

Section 1: A Shepherd's Calling

The story starts with Diocesan Strickland's calling to the ministry — an excursion that flourished in the dirt of Fredericksburg, Texas. From his initial years, the seeds of administration were planted in the rich embroidered artwork of his Catholic childhood. As we investigate the developmental minutes that molded his job, we witness the rise of a shepherd whose calling stretches out a long ways past the safe-haven.

Section 2: Episcopacy and Vision

The story unfurls with Cleric Strickland's arrangement as the fourth priest of the Bishopric of Tyler. As he accepts the episcopal mantle, we dig into his vision for the Congregation — one grounded in the conviction that help isn't bound to ritualistic customs however stretches out into the texture of daily existence. How can he imagine the Congregation's part in serving the more extensive world, and what standards guide his peaceful administration?

Section 3: Building Scaffolds through Service
In this section, we investigate Diocesan Strickland's unmistakable way to deal with associating the Congregation with the more extensive world. Through a bunch of administration drives, local area outreach projects, and associations with neighborhood associations, he turns into an extension developer,

encouraging a significant discourse between the Congregation and the different requirements of society.

Part 4: Difficulties and Controversies

No excursion of administration is without its difficulties. This section explores the discussions that might have emerged as Cleric Strickland took an intense position on moral and doctrinal issues. How could he explore these difficulties, and what effect did they have on his main goal to interface the Congregation with the more extensive world?

Part 5: Tradition of Service

As we finish up, we consider the inheritance Cleric Joseph E. Strickland leaves in the Bishopric of Tyler. How has his obligation to support affected the Congregation's job in the more extensive local area, and what persevering through standards will keep on forming the Congregation's commitment with the world under his significant administration?

This book welcomes you on an excursion — an excursion into the existence of Diocesan Joseph E. Strickland, whose immovable commitment to support has turned into a guide enlightening the way where the hallowed meets the mainstream, and the Congregation reverberates with the more extensive world through extraordinary demonstrations of sympathy and love.

INTRODUCING BISHOP JOSEPH STRICKLAND

Joseph Edward Strickland (conceived October 31, 1958) is an American prelate of the Catholic Church, who was sanctified a diocesan for the Ward of Tyler in eastern Texas in 2012. On November 11, 2023, in an uncommon move, he was eliminated from the post by Pope Francis.

Church

Catholic Church

Bishopric

Bishopric of Tyler

Delegated

September 29, 2012

Introduced

November 28, 2012

Term finished

November 11, 2023

Ancestor

Álvaro Corrada del Río

Replacement

Joe S. Vásquez (Biblical manager)

Orders

Appointment

June 1, 1985

by Thomas Ambrose Tschoepe

Sanctification

November 28, 2012

by Daniel DiNardo, Michael Sheehan, and Álvaro Corrada del Río

Individual subtleties

Conceived

October 31, 1958 (age 65)

Fredericksburg, Texas, U.S.

Training

Heavenly Trinity Theological school

College of Dallas

Catholic College of America

Aphorism

Ut inhabitem in domo Domini

(That I might abide in the place of the Ruler) (Hymn 27:4)

Escutcheon

Joseph Strickland's escutcheon

Styles of

Joseph Edward Strickland

Reference style

His Excellency

The Most Reverend

Spoken style

Your Excellency

Strict style

Minister

History

EARLY LIFE

Joseph Strickland was brought into the world on October 31, 1958, in Fredericksburg, Texas. As a small kid, his family moved to Atlanta, Texas, where his folks were establishing individuals from St. Catherine of Siena Catholic Ward. Strickland went to Sacred Trinity Theological college in Irving, Texas.

Brotherhood

Strickland was appointed to the brotherhood by Cleric Thomas Tschoepe on June 1, 1985, for the See of Dallas. His most memorable task was to Impeccable Origination Area in Tyler, Texas. Upon the formation of the See of Tyler in 1987, Strickland was incardinated, or moved into, the new see and was named its most memorable business chief in Walk 1987 by Diocesan Charles Herzig. Strickland's administration additionally remembered periods at Consecrated Heart Ward for Nacogdoches, Texas and St. Michael Area in Mt. Charming, Texas.

In 1992, Strickland was relegated by Minister Edmond Carmody to concentrate on group regulation at

Catholic College of America in Washington, D.C., where he procured a Licentiate of Standard Regulation in 1994. Getting back to Texas, Strickland was named legal vicar of the see and minister of the Church building of the Perfect Origination. In 1995, he was named a respectable prelate with the title of monsignor by Pope John Paul II.

Strickland filled in as biblical manager of the ward from Walk 2000 until January 2001 when Álvaro Corrada del Río was introduced as the new diocesan. In 2010, Strickland was named vicar general. He served in that limit until being named as a representative of the missional chairman upon Corrada's flight for PuertoRico in 2011

Minister of Tyler

Strickland was designated as cleric of the Ward of Tyler by Pope Benedict XVI on September 29, 2012, and was blessed on November 28, 2012, at Caldwell Hall in Tyler. Cardinal Daniel DiNardo was the celebrant and head consecrator. Strickland is the principal local Texan to head the 33-province bishopric.

He was dependent upon a missional appearance in 2023, obviously engaged around the organization of the see and not his straightforward perspectives on different subjects. A gathering of individuals from the Dicastery for Priests in September of that very year examined a suggestion that Strickland be asked to resign.In an open letter to the dependable of the Bishopric of Tyler, Strickland reported that he wouldn't leave, "since that would be me forsaking the group that I was given charge of by Pope Benedict XVI".

On 11 November 2023, Pope Francis freed Strickland from his post as diocesan from Tyler, selecting Joe Vásquez as missional head in his place.

Governmental issues

On November 4, 2012, days before the 2012 US official political decision, Strickland drove a public convention and petitioning heaven administration in midtown Tyler requesting that the reliable move in the direction of God before the political decision. In a publication composed for the Tyler Morning Transmit, Strickland said:

The crucial bits of insight that used to be regardless ought to be the bedrock of our general public are being tested everyday. I trust the political decision on Nov. 6 carries an extraordinary undertaking to us all as individuals of confidence to solemnly ponder what we accept and how those convictions ought to be exemplified in our regulations and upheld by our chiefs.

In September 2020, Strickland supported a video by Fr. James Altman, a cleric in the See of Lacrosse, who said "You can't be Catholic and be a Liberal." In 2021, Altman's minister, William Callahan of LaCrosse, eliminated Altman from service after he opposed a solicitation to leave.

Sex misuse outrage

In August 2018, Carlo Maria Viganò, Missional Nuncio Emeritus to the US delivered a letter charging a few high-positioning prelates, including Pope Francis, of concealing claims of sexual maltreatment against previous Cardinal Theodore McCarrick, and approaching those mindful, including Francis, to leave. Strickland expressed that he tracked down Viganò's claims "trustworthy". In January 2020, subsequent to meeting with Francis, Strickland said he never concurred with Viganò requiring the Pope's acquiescence and that he was happy with the Blessed See's examination of McCarrick.

Coronavirus pandemic

In May 2020, Strickland marked a request delivered by Viganò which scrutinized limitations during the Coronavirus pandemic as purposefully "making alarm among the total populace with the sole point of for all time monumental unsuitable types of limitation on opportunities." The appeal singles out the utilization of contact following gadgets as well as obligatory immunization as encroachments on individuals' privileges, and refers to "developing questions ... about the genuine infectiousness, risk, and obstruction of the infection."

In a December 2020 letter to his see with respect to the Coronavirus immunizations, Strickland stated "I ask you to dismiss any immunization that utilizes the remaining parts of cut short kids." He later tweeted, "The reality stays that ANY antibody accessible today includes utilizing killed kids before they might actually be conceived." He added, "I recharge my vow — I won't expand my life by Utilizing killed youngsters. This is abhorrent WAKE UP!"

Tridentine Mass

Priest Joseph Strickland observing Conventional Latin Mass, around 2021.

Strickland praised the Tridentine Mass interestingly June 2020, portraying it as respectful and wonderful. Strickland urged Catholics to go to Mass there of the Roman custom, and urged Catholicsattached to the Tridentine Mass to go to the Mass of Paul VI, which he said could likewise be commended respectfully.

LGBT freedoms

Considering a narrative delivered in October 2020, a few proposed this as Pope Francis' communicated help for the legitimization of common associations; Strickland excused the pope's proclamation as only assessment, and said that its delivery was confounding and hazardous.

ROOTS AND ARRANGEMENTS OF BISHOP STRICKLAND

Cleric Joseph E. Strickland's foundations follow back to Fredericksburg, Texas, where he was brought into the world on October 31, 1958. Experiencing childhood in an overwhelmingly Catholic people group, his initial life was formed by the qualities and customs of his confidence. Strickland's family assumed a critical part in encouraging his strict childhood, imparting in him a profound feeling of obligation to the Catholic Church.

In his early stages, Diocesan Strickland went to nearby schools, where his enthusiasm for training and confidence started to entwine. The solid impact of the Catholic people group in Fredericksburg assumed a huge part in sustaining his otherworldly turn of events, in the long run driving him to recognize a work to the organization.

After finishing his underlying training, Strickland sought after additional examinations in philosophy and reasoning, laying the foundation for his future service. This time of scholarly and profound arrangement outfitted him with the information and rules that would shape his way to deal with authority inside the Congregation.

Minister Strickland's excursion toward the organization finished in his appointment in 1985. His underlying foundations in Fredericksburg, set apart by an affectionate Catholic people group and an underpinning of confidence, laid the preparation for a day to day existence committed to serving the Congregation and its lessons. This early climate essentially impacted the qualities and viewpoints that would characterize Cleric Strickland's later job as a shepherd of the Catholic steadfast.

APPOINTMENT AND EARLY SERVICE

Following his appointment as a minister in 1985, Cleric Joseph E. Strickland left on a committed way of service inside the Catholic Church. His initial a very long time as a minister were described by a pledge to serving the otherworldly necessities of the reliable and spreading the lessons of the Catholic confidence.

In the underlying phases of his service, Strickland probably took on different peaceful jobs, drawing in with parishioners, offering direction, and partaking in the sacrosanct existence of the Congregation. These encounters gave him a useful comprehension of the difficulties and delights looked by the Catholic people group at the grassroots level.

As a cleric, Strickland might have been engaged with instructive drives, adding to the scholarly and profound development of those under his consideration. Whether through educating, directing, or partaking in local area occasions, he probably tried to have a constructive outcome on the existences of individuals he served.

These early long periods of service were critical in forming Diocesan Strickland's way to deal with peaceful administration. The encounters acquired during this time would have impacted his viewpoints on the requirements of the Congregation and its individuals, laying the basis for his later job as a diocesan.

The devotion and excitement showed in his initial service were logical demonstrative of the enthusiasm and responsibility that would check Priest Strickland's proceeded with administration to the Congregation. These early stages set up for his possible arrangement as the fourth minister of Tyler in 2012.

EPISCOPAL APPOINTMENT

In 2012, Priest Joseph E. Strickland got a critical and extraordinary arrangement when he was named the fourth cleric of the See of Tyler, Texas. This arrangement denoted a urgent second in his religious process, entrusting him with the peaceful consideration and administration of the Catholic dedicated in the ward.

The choice to delegate Diocesan Strickland to this position probably elaborate cautious thought of his religious keenness, peaceful experience, and obligation to maintaining the lessons of the Catholic Church. His standing for adherence to conventional qualities and solid promotion for Catholic precept might have figured into the choice, lining up with the necessities and assumptions for the diocesan local area.

After expecting the job of diocesan, Strickland would have assumed the obligations of shepherding the dependable, managing the organization of the bishopric, and giving profound direction to both pastorate and common people. His administration style, formed by his prior years in service and his obligation to the standards of the Catholic confidence, started to make an unmistakable imprint on the Ward of Tyler.

The Episcopal arrangement addressed another section in Diocesan Strickland's life and service, offering him a stage to additional impact and shape the direction of the Catholic Church in East Texas. His residency as cleric would be described by a devotion to conventional qualities, promotion for Catholic lessons, and a peaceful methodology pointed toward encouraging the profound prosperity of the diocesan local area.

ADMINISTRATION STYLE AND VALUES

Diocesan Joseph E. Strickland is known for an initiative style portrayed by areas of strength for a to customary Catholic qualities and steady adherence to doctrinal standards. His initiative mirrors a moderate methodology, underscoring the conservation of customary lessons inside the setting of the Catholic confidence.

1. Doctrinal Adherence:

- Priest Strickland's initiative is set apart by an unfaltering obligation to maintaining standard Catholic principles. He advocates for loyalty to the lessons of the Congregation, particularly on issues of ethical quality and religious philosophy.

2. Peaceful Concern:

- His initiative style integrates a peaceful worry for the otherworldly prosperity of the Catholic dependable. Strickland is probably going to focus on peaceful consideration, meaning to guide and support the individuals from his ward in their confidence process.

3. Customary Values:

- Priest Strickland is known for supporting customary Catholic qualities, upholding for the significance of these qualities in contemporary society. This incorporates issues connected with family, sacredness of life, and adherence to moral lessons.

4. Backing for Social Justice:

- While underscoring conventional qualities, Strickland is probably going to address civil rights issues inside the structure of Catholic lessons. This might include pushing for the minimized and defenseless, in arrangement with the standards of Catholic social convention.

5. Clear Communication:

- His authority style probably includes clear and direct correspondence, giving direction on issues of confidence and profound quality. Priest Strickland may effectively draw in with the Catholic people group, ministry, and the more extensive public to verbalize his perspectives and lessons.

6. Customary Liturgy:

- Cleric Strickland's initiative may likewise reach out to an inclination for conventional ritualistic practices inside the Catholic Church. He might advocate for the conservation of ceremonial customs that line up with the verifiable acts of the Congregation.

In outline, Diocesan Strickland's administration is described by a strong obligation to conventional

Catholic qualities, a peaceful worry for the prosperity of the reliable, and an unmistakable and direct correspondence style. His methodology mirrors a commitment to saving the doctrinal respectability of the Catholic confidence while tending to contemporary difficulties considering customary lessons.

CONTENTIONS AND PROMOTION

Cleric Joseph E. Strickland has been associated with different contentions and has been a vocal supporter for explicit moral and doctrinal situations inside the Catholic Church. A few eminent examples include:

1. Doctrinal Controversies:

- Diocesan Strickland has been known to areas of strength for offer on doctrinal issues, particularly those connected with issues of confidence and profound quality. His blunt position on specific philosophical points could have prompted discussions and contentions inside the more extensive Church people group.

2. Moral Teachings:

- Strickland is a backer for customary Catholic moral lessons. This remembers his firm position for issues like the holiness of life, marriage, and family values. His backing here might have ignited conversations and discussions both inside and outside the Catholic people group.

3. Social Issues:

- The cleric might have participated in debates connected with social issues, tending to them according to a Catholic viewpoint. This could include issues like destitution, movement, or medical care, where Strickland's perspectives line up with customary Catholic social teaching.

4. Formal Practices:

   - Priest Strickland's promotion for customary ritualistic practices might have mixed banters inside the Congregation people group. Conversations about the harmony between saving custom and adjusting to contemporary practices might have arisen in this unique circumstance.

5. Public Statements:

   - His public assertions, whether through interviews, virtual entertainment, or peaceful letters, could have produced debate because of the frankness with which he communicates his perspectives. Discussions could emerge when his assertions address delicate or discussed subjects.

6. Religious Governance:

  - Priest Strickland's way to deal with clerical administration and his perspectives on the construction of the Congregation might have prompted conversations and discussions, particularly assuming his points of view vary from winning feelings inside the Congregation ordered progression.

It's vital to take note of that while discussions exist, Priest Strickland's promotion is attached in his obligation to customary Catholic lessons. Contentions frequently emerge major areas of strength for when on doctrinal or moral issues challenge winning social or cultural standards.

PASTORAL WORK AND OUTREACH

Cleric Joseph E. Strickland has been effectively participated in peaceful work and effort, showing a guarantee to the profound prosperity and improvement of the Catholic people group. A few parts of his peaceful endeavors might include:

1. Holy Ministry:

- Effectively taking part in and managing the organization of ceremonies, including Mass, compromise, and other formal festivals, to encourage the profound existence of the dependable.

2. Peaceful Care:

- Giving peaceful consideration to the individuals from his see, offering direction, backing, and profound insight to people and families confronting different difficulties.

3. Instruction and Formation:

- Stressing training and arrangement by supporting drives that advance the scholarly and otherworldly development of the Catholic people group, including catechesis projects, schools, and grown-up confidence arrangement.

4. Local area Engagement:

- Effectively captivating with the nearby local area, taking part in occasions, and cultivating a feeling of local area among parishioners. This might include going to ward social affairs, festivities, and local area outreach programs.

5. Civil rights Initiatives:

- Pushing for civil rights issues lined up with Catholic lessons, for example, tending to destitution, advancing the poise of each and every human individual, and supporting drives that add to the benefit of all.

6. Family and Marriage Support:

- Offering peaceful help to families and advancing the sacredness of marriage and everyday life. This could include giving assets, arranging withdraws, or tending to contemporary difficulties confronting families.

7. Proselytizing Efforts:

- Effectively partaking in and elevating proselytizing endeavors to impart the Catholic confidence to both the Catholic people group and those external the Congregation.

8. Altruistic Work:

- Supporting and empowering altruistic drives, incorporating associations with neighborhood associations to address the requirements of the less lucky and minimized in the public eye.

Minister Strickland's peaceful work and effort probably mirror a comprehensive way to deal with shepherding the Catholic dependable, enveloping profound, instructive, and social aspects. Through these endeavors, he intends to fortify the securities inside the confidence local area and contribute decidedly to the more extensive society.

INFLUENCE ON THE DIOCESE

Cleric Joseph E. Strickland fundamentally affects the See of Tyler, Texas, through his initiative and peaceful endeavors. A few critical parts of his effect on the see include:

1. Doctrinal Clarity:

   - Minister Strickland's accentuation on doctrinal clearness and devotion to Catholic lessons has likely added to a fortified feeling of religious character inside the ward.

2. Profound Formation:

- His obligation to schooling and profound development might have prompted a more educated and profoundly drew in Catholic people group, with drives supporting both youth and grown-up confidence development.

3. Peaceful Care:

- Through dynamic peaceful consideration, Minister Strickland plays probably had an impact in supporting people and families inside the bishopric, giving direction during huge life altering situations and difficulties.

4. Local area Unity:

- The cleric's contribution in local area commitment and effort drives might have encouraged a more prominent feeling of solidarity and fellowship among the Catholic reliable in the see.

5. Customary Values:

- Strickland's backing for conventional Catholic qualities might have reverberated with a section of the diocesan local area, adding to a feeling of coherence with the verifiable lessons of the Congregation.

6. Social Impact:

- Through civil rights drives and beneficent work, the see might decidedly affect the more extensive local area, resolving cultural issues and adding to the benefit of all.

7. Ceremonial Practices:

- The minister's help for conventional ceremonial practices might have impacted how ceremony is praised inside the see, adding to a feeling of congruity with verifiable Catholic love.

8. Proselytizing Efforts:

- Strickland's accentuation on proselytizing might have prompted expanded outreach endeavors, carrying the Catholic confidence to those inside the see and cultivating a teacher soul among the unwavering.

By and large, Diocesan Strickland's effect on the Ward of Tyler is logical multi-layered, enveloping otherworldly, peaceful, and local area aspects. The particular nature and degree of this effect would rely upon the remarkable conditions and difficulties looked by the ward during his residency.

REFLECTIONS AND HERITAGE

As Priest Joseph E. Strickland's residency unfurls, his appearance and heritage inside the Catholic Church become progressively critical:

1. Doctrinal Legacy:

- Strickland's enduring obligation to doctrinal universality is probably going to leave an enduring heritage, impacting how the Ward of Tyler draws near and deciphers Catholic lessons.

2. Peaceful Emphasis:

- On the off chance that his peaceful accentuation perseveres, it could shape the see's continuous obligation to giving otherworldly direction, peaceful consideration, and cultivating a feeling of local area among its individuals.

3. Instructive Impact:

- Priest Strickland's emphasis on schooling and otherworldly development might add to a tradition of very much educated and profoundly drew in Catholics inside the ward.

4. Civil rights Advocacy:

- In the event that his support for civil rights issues is proceeded, the ward could sustainedly affect tending to cultural difficulties and advancing Catholic social lessons.

5. Ceremonial Traditions:

- Strickland's help for customary ceremonial practices might impact the ward's way to deal with love, adding to a tradition of respect for verifiable ritualistic customs.

6. Solidarity and Local area Building:

- His endeavors towards local area commitment and solidarity might bring about an enduring tradition of a closely knit and strong Catholic people group inside the ward.

7. Challenges and Controversies:

- Contingent upon the idea of any difficulties or discussions during his residency, they might shape the bishopric's way to deal with tending to and exploring such issues from here on out.

8. Proselytizing and Outreach:

- On the off chance that his accentuation on proselytizing perseveres, the see might proceed to effectively share the Catholic confidence and draw in with the more extensive local area, adding to a tradition of evangelist outreach.

Eventually, Priest Strickland's inheritance will be a powerful exchange of these elements, impacted by the ward's reaction to his initiative and the more extensive setting of the Catholic Church. Reflections on his effect will keep on advancing as the ward explores the authentic steadily changing scene and society.

COAT OF ARMS OF JOSEPH STRICKLAND

The emblem was planned and embraced when he was selected as the Minister of Tyler.

Taken on

28 November 2012

Crest

The left side is the escutcheon of the Bishopric of Tyler. The right side incorporates at the top are the Holy Heart and the Faultless Heart, the shell addresses the Strickland family peak and is additionally in Pope Benedict XVI's crest. The wavy line is taken from the emblem of the Bishopric of Dallas where he contemplated and was appointed to the brotherhood. The cross of stars addresses the

Southern Cross which is apparent in Australia and is important for the Australian banner.

Witticism

UT INHABITEM IN DOMO DOMINI (Song 27:4)

CONCLUSION

All in all, Priest Joseph E. Strickland's initiative inside the Bishopric of Tyler has left an unmistakable engraving on the Catholic people group. Through an undaunted obligation to doctrinal universality, a peaceful spotlight on the profound prosperity of the unwavering, and an accentuation on conventional qualities, he has molded the direction of the bishopric.

His heritage incorporates a mix of doctrinal lucidity, peaceful consideration, instructive drives, and a guarantee to civil rights. The effect of Priest Strickland's residency stretches out past the diocesan limits, impacting how the Congregation draws in with contemporary difficulties while residual established in its rich practice.

As the see ponders Minister Strickland's authority, the persevering through heritage will be found in the fortified feeling of character, solidarity, and mission among the Catholic reliable. The difficulties confronted, discussions explored, and the steps made in peaceful, instructive, and social undertakings altogether add to the enduring tradition of Priest Joseph E. Strickland inside the See of Tyler.

www.ingramcontent.com/pod-product-compliance
Lightning Source LLC
LaVergne TN
LVHW021412220525
811970LV00009B/291